D1379218

Early Settler Children

Bobbie Kalman

The Early Settler Life Series

 Crabtree Publishing Company

To my dear friends, the Baudes: André, Elisabeth, Olivia, Adrien, Erika, and Jacques

A very special thanks to:

My excellent editorial, research, and layout staff:
Lise Gunby, Nancy Cook, and Rosemary McLernon.

The expert photographers who are responsible for the faithful reproductions of historical materials:
Sarah Peters and Stephen Mangione.

The librarians and historians who were so cooperative in providing me with historical materials and photographic opportunities:
William Loos, Margaret Crawford Maloney, Dana Tenny, Jill Shefrin, Christine Castle, and Margaret Perkins

My models: *Andrea Crabtree, Lise Gunby, and Margaret Perkins.*

Cataloging in Publication Data

Kalman, Bobbie, 1947 –
  Early Settler Children

(Early settler life series)
Includes index.
ISBN   0-86505-019-8 hardcover
ISBN   0-86505-018-X softcover

1. Children – History.   2. Children – Social conditions
I. Title.   II. Series

HQ 767. 87. K 33   305. 2' 3' 09   LC93-6182

350 Fifth Ave, Suite 3308
New York, NY 10118

R.R. #4
360 York Road
Niagara-on-the-Lake, ON
Canada L0S 1J0

73 Lime Walk
Headington, Oxford 0X3 7AD
United Kingdom

Contents

Just like you

Settler children were just like you in many ways. They were born needing love, security, nourishment, companionship, happiness, and adventure. They had the same feelings that you have, the same needs, and many of the same dreams. But their lives were different from yours. They grew up in a different kind of world.

4

Everyone in this settler home had jobs to do. Crops had to be grown and harvested. Animals had to be fed and cared for. Bread and butter had to be made from scratch.

A different way of showing love

In this book we will explore what it was like to be a child in settler times. We will meet settler children at work and at play. We will find out how their parents treated them. The settlers had different ideas from ours about how children should be brought up. Loving your child meant raising him or her to become a good human being. Parents thought children had to learn right from wrong at a very early age. There was no room for mischief. Life was taken very seriously. If a parent allowed a child to misbehave or be lazy, that parent felt he or she was not a good parent. However, parents did feel love for their children. The feelings were the same, even if the ways of showing love might have been quite different.

Parents took their duties as parents seriously. They wanted their children to be well-behaved, quiet, and obedient. They needed their children to be hard workers. All these ideas prevented children from being "just kids."

Pulling their weight

In our society today, people feel that children should grow into adults slowly. Children are expected to have plenty of time for play as well as for school. In settler times, things were different. There was so much work to be done in the New World. Land had to be cleared, shelters built, and crops planted. Often the climate was harsh, and everyone, from the oldest to the youngest, had to lend a hand so the new community could survive.

Children were no exception to the rule that everyone had to work. Parents expected them to behave more as responsible "little adults" than as carefree, fun-loving children. They needed their children to help around the home or on the farm, or to go out and earn wages as soon as possible. Parents felt that children should contribute to their family's success in any way they could. Being young was no excuse for being idle. Often it must have seemed to the children that they were loved only as much as they were able to work.

This extended family was made up of a mother, father, grandmother, and two children. Each family member had a special role to play.

Under the same roof

Today, when we use the word "family," we usually mean a mother and father and their children living together under one roof. In settler times, the word "family" had a larger meaning. Children, their parents and grandparents, and even their uncles and aunts, shared the same home. Today, we describe this arrangement as an "extended family."

One way that the settlers made sure that such a large group of adults and children could live together happily was to have firm ideas about how everyone within the group should behave. Each person knew exactly what role he or she was expected to play.

Strict rules for behavior did more than just help people live together peacefully in large groups. In a country where there was so much that was new and different, the settlers were able to feel more secure and safe when some things stayed the same. For example, they kept their old ideas about how children should behave. Maybe today we accept change more readily.

You may find it strange when we say something such as "Boys were expected to ..." or "Girls usually did ..." Today boys and girls do the same things. Both mothers and fathers look after children. Sometimes a mother goes to work outside the home while a father looks after the house. Also, there may be one parent who brings up the family, rather than two. In settler times, these different ways of doing things did not seem right, or even possible.

In the early days most of the outdoor work was done by the father. In the picture above the father of the household is a fisherman. His sons will probably grow up to be fishermen too. Mother and her two sons wait for Father to return with the day's catch.

Fathers taught their sons how to tame horses, break in steers, yoke oxen, and herd cattle. The father's role in the home was to be the head of the family. His decision was law.

Mothers were expected to be firm, but also gentle with their children. Their role in the settler home was to do all the domestic jobs, such as cooking, baking, and cleaning, and to raise their children with love.

"Spare the rod and spoil the child"

The expression "spare the rod and spoil the child" was taken seriously by the settlers. Parents believed that if their children misbehaved, they should be punished immediately and harshly. The father, above, may have to "spare the rod" until later. His son would rather jump in the lake than be beaten.

Children were punished for many reasons. The boy, above, is using his father's brush and razor. He will probably get a beating for not asking first.

Suzie has to stand in the corner for an hour. Her mother caught her outside while she was supposed to be napping.

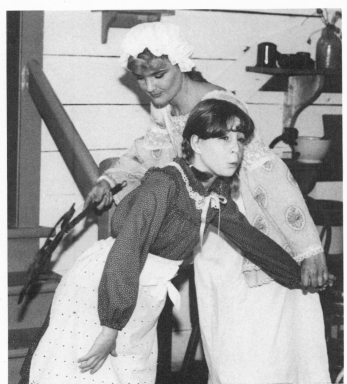

Andrea is getting an old-fashioned spanking with a carpet-beater.

Mark decided to try his father's pipe. His father was not pleased. What do you think Mark's punishment might be?

The grandmother in this picture is also the storekeeper. Her two granddaughters love to spend much of their time with her in the store. Because she is the storekeeper, this grandmother knows everyone in the village. She is a very wise and important person, not only to her family, but to the whole community.

Wisdom and love from Grandma and Grandpa

The grandparents took charge of teaching the children about God. They read the Bible to the smaller children. They listened to the older children recite the Scriptures. The grandmother was often the healer in the family. She knew all about herbs. She could make tonics to prevent or cure illnesses. Everyone in the settler family respected the grandparents for their knowledge and experience of life. Advice given by the grandparents was usually followed.

Bessie loves to hear the news from faraway places. Grandfather keeps the whole family up-to-date on the latest developments. He reads the newspapers from cover to cover.

Grandpa plays the accordion while Wilma does a jig. Wilma is very happy that her grandfather lives with her. They are best friends.

Grandmother cuddles Serena. With grandparents in the house, there is always someone to pay attention to a little girl or boy.

Bubbling with baby facts

The settlers wanted to have as many children as possible. Each new baby brought joy to the settler household. The more children a person had, the more helping hands there were to run the farm or the family business.

When a woman was expecting a baby she was told to think only sweet thoughts. People believed that ugly thoughts would somehow harm the baby.

The role of the godparent was a very important one. Godparents were expected to care for the children in the case of the parents' deaths. Godparents were always welcome in the child's home. They offered the parents advice on bringing up the child.

The settlers' babies were not born in a hospital. They were born at home. There was a room in the house named "the borning room," where the babies entered the world. This room was usually beside the kitchen where it was quite warm.

Parents in those days did not tell their children how a baby was born. Children thought storks brought babies. Some children even believed that babies were found under cabbage leaves.

Popular names for girls were Sarah, Mary, Faith, Hope, Patience, and Charity. When a child was named after a relative or friend, an adjective was usually added to the name. The child was then called "little Joe" or "smiling Sarah."

Following the birth of a baby, neighbors sent cards to the new mother. The mother returned thank-you cards to those who had asked about the baby. When the mother was strong enough to have visitors, she invited her friends and neighbors to come and see the new offspring. Gentlemen were not supposed to visit the new mother and child until much later.

The neighbors gave the mother gifts of homemade items for the baby. The godmother often gave the christening dress and cap as her present. The godfather either gave the child a Bible or a gift of silver, such as a baby cup or spoon.

When a baby was born, he or she was given a wine bath. People believed that wine would make the baby strong. The baby was then wrapped in flannel.

The most popular names for children were taken from the Bible. Boys were called Joshua, Joseph, Peter, John, Noah, Daniel, Matthew, and Abraham.

The first duty of a parent was to have the new baby baptized as soon as it was possible. The godparents were chosen soon after the baby was born.

Baby love

Everyone welcomed new babies into the household. Each new child meant another person to help with the work. Soon after this baby learned to walk, she had to pull her weight doing household chores.

Baby Louise

I'm in love with you, Baby Louise!
With your silken hair and your soft blue
eyes,
And the dreamy wisdom that in them lies;
And the faint, sweet smile you brought
from the skies,
God's sunshine, Baby Louise.

When you fold your hands, Baby Louise,
Your hands, like a fairy's so tiny and
fair,
With a pretty, innocent, saint-like air,
Are you trying to think of some angel-
taught prayer,
You learned above, Baby Louise?

*Babies slept in all kinds of cradles. Some
rocked, some swung from side to side.
Some children slept in dresser drawers
or benches instead of cradles.*

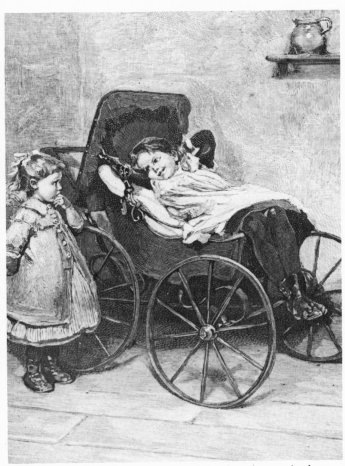

*These little girls are remembering their
baby days. Most settler babies were
not lucky enough to have had carriages
because they were expensive.*

*Mothers loved their newborn babies.
Babies were cute and cuddly. However,
very soon this mother will start to
discipline more and cuddle less.*

Pinafores, diapers, bonnets, and bows

Babies were dressed in diapers, a flannel petticoat, and a dress. This child will soon be old enough to wear the same type of clothes her mother wears. She already has buttoned shoes similar to her mother's.

Edith is wearing her best clothes. She has on a fancy bonnet and a lacy cape with a huge bow.

In the winter Edith wears a loose dress made of heavy material. A white lace collar sits on top of a satin one.

This baby has just been christened. His christening dress is about three times as long as he is. A christening was a very important event. Most of the community turned up with beautiful gifts for the baby.

One might think that Sydney is a girl because of the way he is dressed. In settler times both boys and girls wore dresses. Sydney is wearing a cotton pinafore over his dress. Pinafores kept dresses from getting dirty.

17

Dressed up as little adults

The well-to-do settlers dressed their children in fancy dresses, huge hats, and furry coats and muffs. These clothes may look appealing, but they did not allow the child to run or play. Not only were children dressed to look like little adults, they were expected to act like little adults. Running and playing were not considered "proper" behavior.

Boys grew their hair long and wore skirts until the age of six or seven. The parents of these boys came from Scotland. The boys are wearing Scottish kilts.

The child in this old photograph does not look very comfortable. Her bonnet and coat are made of stiff, heavy material. This type of clothing was not suitable for chasing a frisky dog.

Samantha is wearing her Sunday-best clothes. She has a large straw hat, just like her mother's. Her clothes were made of the same material as those of her mother.

There are two girls and a boy in this picture. The hairstyles and clothing of all these children are almost the same. Often very young boys and girls wore the same clothes.

Even the youngest children in the settler household had jobs to do. Barbara washes Donald's face in the morning. She looks after him throughout the day.

Love your work!

Silly people don't like to work,
Let us try to love it;
Grave and great ones of the land
They are not above it.

Lazy people all get dull,
Mind and body weary;
Waking ones grow strong and bright
Time is never dreary.

Elder sisters, you may work,
Work and help your mothers,
Darn the stockings, mend the shirts,
Father's things and brother's.

Younger sisters, you may help,
Help by minding baby.
Little hands and little feet
Very useful may be.

20

Both boys and girls were taught to knit. Boys knitted their own suspenders. Girls knitted scarves, mittens, stockings, and hats for the whole family.

Girls learned to sew by the age of four. They were able to make their own aprons, slips, and dresses. The little girl, above, is making a dress for her doll.

No excuse for laziness

One of the reasons the settlers wanted to have many children was so that the children could help with all the work that had to be done around the home. Children were taught that laziness was the worst sin of all. Children had to rise early in the morning and make themselves useful before going to school. After school they had to return straight home and finish other chores before supper. Children were punished if they complained about having to do a job. They were not allowed to say they were tired.

Everyone in the family learned to sew. Men and boys learned to sew simple stitches. They could put up hems and sew on buttons. Girls learned to sew many different stitches. They learned these stitches by making "samplers." Samplers were made to show off a girl's ability to do needlework. Samplers usually contained the letters of the alphabet. They also contained verses from the Bible. Samplers taught the alphabet and simple stitches at the same time. When a sampler was finished, it was framed. The name and age of the person who made it were sewn on as well.

A sampler made by a young girl in 1816. The lines have no punctuation. The first three lines say, "Jesu permit thy name to stand as the first effort of an infant's hand and as Her fingers on the canvas move incline her heart to seek thy love with Thy dear people let her have a part O write thy name thy love upon her heart."

Picking berries was a job both boys and girls loved to do. It gave young people a chance to talk and get to know one another. These young people are working at Mr. Martin's farm for a month. The extra money they earn will help out their families.

These children are having fun hunting for eggs. The chickens have laid them everywhere! John shows Tom his latest find. It was hidden in the straw.

Bringing in kindling, wood chips, and wood for burning was a job for both boys and girls.

These children look after a newborn calf. They try to make him drink some water.

Chores for boys and girls

Some of the chores done by both boys and girls were: picking berries, feeding the animals, gathering fruit and vegetables, dipping candles, collecting eggs, and bringing in kindling and firewood. A young settler described how she once tried to cut corners on a chore. Her job was to gather the wood chips that had fallen to the ground where her father was chopping logs for firewood. She was then supposed to dry them in the oven. The wood chips were to be used in starting the fire the following morning.

Wet wood kindles fiery temper

"One day, careless little animal that I was, I gathered my chips, but paying no heed to drying them in the oven, just flopped them on the kitchen floor and went off to bed .... On this particular morning, the kindling was damp. The fire would not light. It smoldered and went out twice. My father's patience wore out. His anger flared up, if the fire did not. It was six o'clock on a bleak winter's morning when the crack of doom overtook me. I was lying snug and warm, fast asleep. After having been yanked out of my cosy bed, a swift and thoroughly deserved spanking was my fate!"

The little girl in the story was not surprised at her punishment. She even felt that she deserved it. She learned the hard way that one did not cheat on doing one's chores.

Young farmhands

Jim looks on as his father and uncle try to tame a wild horse. It will be his job to train the horse to pull the family's sleigh.

"Breaking in" a pair of calves was Johnny's chore for the day. The calves had to learn to walk and work together with a yoke around their necks.

Father teaches his sons to cut the hay "straight and clean" with the scythe.

Jeff's job is to herd cattle. Jeff's family owns several hundred steers. Jeff will someday run the ranch.

It was usually a girl's job to look after the younger members of the family. Sally is careful that the sheep don't hurt her baby sister.

Yvonne helps Mother to cook supper for the family. She is peeling potatoes and onions for a stew.

Andrea irons her apron with a flatiron. She heated the iron first by placing it next to the fire in the fireplace.

Domestic chores

Most of the jobs in the home were done by women and girls. From a very early age girls learned to spin, weave, make candles and soap, sew, bake bread, make butter and cheese, and cook. Girls were also responsible for cleaning the house and washing the dishes. A young prairie girl of nine described how she received some unexpected help with her chore one day. Adela was about to begin her nightly job of washing dishes. She was excited that evening because a young soldier had stopped by the house. Her aunt invited him in for supper. While they were eating he told them wonderful stories about faraway places. After supper he and Adela's aunt went to the parlor to continue their conversation. Adela was left alone to do the dishes. This is what happened next.

26

"Over went the show." The tub tipped and the water ran all over the floor. Auntie was ready to box Adela's ears.

Dishwashing — a disaster!

"The water and the soap were in the dish tub, which was placed on the edge of the table. When I raised my hands to put in the pile of plates, I somehow hit something. Over went the show – that is, the dish tub of hot water, for I still held the plates in my hand. My scream brought Auntie and the soldier from the next room. They were both out before the water had run a quarter of the way over the floor. Auntie's temper was like a good pie crust - very short. She raised her hand to box my ears, but quick as she was, that young soldier was quicker still. A very large hand came from behind and caught her wrist, and a very loud, cheery voice said, 'No, no, you must not! The poor little Siss, she wasn't tall enough to reach over the tub.'

"Then everything happened together. Through the magnifying and multiplying lenses of my tears the floor seemed covered with arms, hands, legs, boots, spurs, and shiny buttons. The ceiling rang with roaring laughter as that soldier man mopped up the water and wrung out the dishcloth and cleaned up the floor in the twinkling of an eye. Then he jumped to his feet and clicked his spurs, and tickled me under the chin. 'No more tears, Siss,' he said, 'I'll wash your dishes for you.' And he did - while he whistled and whooped and sang soldiers' songs. The very harness on the walls trembled with joy. After that he kept me by his knee telling stories. Then he mounted his horse and rode away, waving his hat high over his head and yo-hoing at me. We never knew his name or whence he came or whither he went. The bright vision of his kindness never faded from my memory. He restored me to complete happiness and cheery pleasure in the midst of one of my most unpleasant chores."

Nancy is the postmaster's daughter. She waits for the train to pick up the mail. She and her dog, Licorice, will exchange this pouch for one containing letters for the villagers.

Sharing the family business

Not all the settler children had farmers as parents. Some of the settlers were gristmill or sawmill owners, storekeepers, craftspeople, such as blacksmiths or coopers, bakers, clockmakers, and printers. The children of the business-people had different chores to do. They helped their parents before and after school. For example, the children of the storekeeper served the customers, dusted shelves, and helped to weigh the groceries. The miller's son and daughter helped by weighing the flour, loading and unloading farmers' wagons, and sweeping floors.

David and Harry help their father after school. Their father is a fisherman. Both David and Harry are already good at catching fish.

Douglas is the miller's son. He helps his father unload sacks of grain. He also sweeps the floors, weighs the flour, and helps the customers who come to the mill.

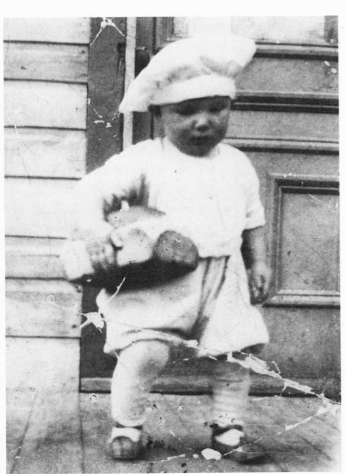

Tim is already working at the age of two. His father is a baker. Tim is delivering a loaf of bread to the blacksmith.

Rita is learning to be a blacksmith. Her father owns the village shop. Rita is pounding out a horseshoe. Her favorite job is shoeing horses.

Running off to sea

The boys who lived near the sea coast or the shores of the bigger lakes and rivers dreamed of running off to sea to become sailors. The following is the story of a brave sailor boy who nearly gave up his life to save his captain. His heroic deed did not go unrewarded.

The courageous little sailor

A schooner was suddenly struck by a heavy gust of wind, upset, and instantly sunk. A vessel nearby, which had seen the disaster, sent its boat to save any survivors from sinking. On coming nearer to where the schooner went down, they saw a little boy twelve years old floating on some wood. As they approached him, he exclaimed, "Never mind me, save the captain; he has a wife and six children."

The kind-hearted boy knew that the captain's family loved him, and would need his support. Happily, both the captain and the boy were saved.

Three days after the vessel was lost, the boy got into a railroad car. As he was poor and ragged, some of the passengers who wore fine clothes shrunk away from him. He took his seat quietly, and the sea captain, who had entered the car with him, told a minister what had happened. The captain added, "The boy has only the clothes you see, sir, or he would not be so ragged. I care not much for myself, though I too lost all; but the poor lad will have a hard time of it."

Several people who heard the story gave the poor orphan small sums of money, and advised him to tell others what he had gone through. They would, no doubt, give him something. Many boys in his situation would have readily taken the advice, and told the story of their misfortunes in order to get help. But the poor boy replied, "I am not a beggar; I don't wish to beg their money."

A gentleman then arose, and pleaded the case of the boy in such a manner, that the passengers gave ten dollars for him. The man who obtained this sum for the unfortunate boy had been a sailor himself. He knew how to pity those in distress because he too had suffered much in his lifetime.

Many homeless boys headed for the ports to work as sailors. They had to work hard, but there was always excitement.

The captain told the passengers about the courage of the sailor boy.

The small stowaways

Not all orphans were able to run away to sea. There were many children on land who had to roam the countryside or the streets of early cities looking for food and shelter. Even as these children struggled to find food, other homeless children stowed away on ships coming from Europe in the hope of finding a home in the New World. It was difficult enough to survive an ocean crossing at the best of times. The chances were even slimmer when one had to hide from the ship's mates. The sailors who worked on these big ships were known for being mean. They terrified even the adult passengers. It was not unusual for these sailors to throw stowaways overboard. That was nearly the fate of one little stowaway.

Menaced by a mean mate

A small boy was discovered on the fourth day of a ship's voyage from Liverpool to New York. One of the ship's mates found him hiding behind some barrels in the ship's hold. He told the mate that he was put on the ship by his stepfather who no longer wanted to look after him. His mother was dead and his only living relative, an aunt, was living in Halifax. His stepfather would not pay for his fare, nor would he allow the boy to stay with him. The boy had no choice. The mate was angry. He thought one of the young sailors smuggled the boy onto the ship. He told the boy, "You have until sundown to tell me which scoundrel brought you aboard this ship. Then if you are still sticking with your make-believe story about your stepfather, you will be thrown overboard as sure as I'm standing here."

Hours later, as the sun was going down, the passengers and sailors crowded on the deck. The mate asked the boy once again, "Who brought you on board this ship?" The boy did not change his story.

He begged the mate for a chance to pray before he was thrown to the sharks. As he knelt down, he prayed to his mother in heaven. He told her how his stepfather had put him on the ship. The passengers wept for the boy. They saw that he had been telling the truth. He was saved. A kind family offered to take the boy to join his aunt.

Some orphans from Europe came to the New World as stowaways on big ships. They risked their lives in the hope of finding a home.

"My stepfather put me on board this ship."

31

There were thousands of homeless children in the nineteenth century. Many came to North America with their parents, but their parents later died from disease or accidents. Orphanages opened to provide children with food, shelter, and the hope of adoption.

The children in this old picture discovered a child sleeping on the other side of the fence. He had been roaming the country-side searching for a home.

People came to orphanages to "adopt" children. But some people just wanted these children for the work they would do. The person who ran this orphanage worried about how these children would be treated in their new homes.

Children without homes

At first there were no orphanages for children who had lost their parents. In the country, children who did not have homes were usually put to work. People in the community hired them and paid them enough to live on in return. Children were also taken in as boarders by people in the community. They worked for their keep. This way of providing for orphans was called *indenture*. Many people were worried about this system because children were treated as slaves by some people.

Almshouses for the poor and homeless

Indenture was not the only way to look after orphans. Gradually *almshouses* were opened. Both adults and children lived in almshouses together. There were more almshouses in the city than in the country. There were more people in the city to run the almshouses as well as to live in them. City children were sent to them if they were caught begging. Children stayed in the almshouses until

someone offered to give them jobs as *apprentices* or servants. Boys were usually sent to work on farms. Girls were sent to do housework for families.

In the nineteenth century, orphanages opened especially for homeless children. In orphanages children were given a little schooling and later sent out as apprentices or servants.

Adoption

In the early days, people who wanted to adopt children arranged their own adoptions. Children who needed homes were advertised in newspapers. Sometimes doctors and nurses told couples about children who could be adopted. Children without parents were also sent from England so that homes could be found for them. They waited in orphanages until they were adopted. When adoption laws were passed, judges in the courts had to agree to adoptions before they were considered legal.

City orphans faced hard times

These boys are "street boys." They have no place to live. They beg for their food. They steal if they have to. The bigger towns and cities were filled with children just like them.

Some cities had "soup kitchens" to provide hungry orphans with food. These children went twice a day for some thin soup and perhaps a piece of bread.

A few orphans were able to earn enough money for food by shining shoes.

Cities were filled with newsboys. Selling papers was another way for orphans to earn a few pennies.

These orphans carry their possessions with them everywhere. Mary owns a blanket which keeps them warm at night. George has a broken-down umbrella for both rainy and sunny days.

If there were no shoes to shine or newspapers to sell, one could always try to sell matches. One boy tells another his secret for making a quick sale.

These boys are plotting to steal food from the grocery store across the road. If they are caught, they will face going to jail. There were no reformatories in the early days.

Children were even sent to jail for small offences such as trespassing. The jails were dirty, crowded, and filled with hardened criminals. A boy, such as the one in the picture, would have no chance to improve in such a place.

Schools for children with disabilities opened in the nineteenth century. People discovered that children with handicaps could learn as well as other children, if they were taught in special ways. These blind boys are able to "see" their work by feeling with their hands.

The punishment was a "crime"

In the early settler days, children who broke the law could be sent to jail. There were no *reformatories* for these children. They went to the same jails as adults did. Most judges tried hard *not* to send young children to adult jails, but sometimes there was no other place for them to go. In one case, a twelve-year-old boy was sent to jail for three years because he stole jewelry.

Jailers did not know what to do with children in their jails. Some jailers "bound out" children who had been sent to them. When children were "bound out," they were sent out to work for their keep. The person they worked for paid the jailer. The jailer needed the money to run the jail and to feed the prisoners.

Ragged schools for ragged children

Finally, reformatories were built. They were also called "ragged schools." The children who lived in ragged schools were not all criminals. Orphans, poor children, and children whose parents did not look after them were also sent to reformatories or ragged schools.

Some ragged schools were only for poor children who had families. The children came to the school during the day and went home to their parents at night. They ate their three meals each day at the ragged school. Most of the day was spent working. The children made furniture, leather items, or clothes. The things they made were sold, and the money went toward paying for the school. After work the children were taught lessons in reading, writing, and arithmetic.

Here is the true story of Andrew, who was sent to a ragged school and who was happier because of it.

Better than home

Andrew's mother dragged him into court and told the judge she wanted him to be put into a reformatory. She complained that Andrew was a wicked child and had hit her. The judge did not want to act hastily. He asked the mother many questions. In the end, he found out that she wanted to marry a man who would not marry her if he had to look after Andrew. The judge could not send Andrew home with his mother, but did not want to send him to a reformatory. There was nowhere else for Andrew to go, however, so the judge sent him to the best ragged school in the district. Andrew found the place so much better than his unhappy home had been that he soon became the best worker and student.

Ah no! I hear the heavy factory bell,
Which takes its sound from factory noise
and din,

And wearily workers respond to its call,
For now a day of hardship must begin.

Child labor

Boys as young as nine years old worked as mule boys in the mines. Mules pulled cars of ore from lower levels. There were no laws against child labor in the early nineteenth century. Children worked ten hours a day for six days each week.

These brickyard workers earn only a few pennies a week for their hard labor. Today, people would be shocked to see children working so hard. In the early days, many people expected children to work at difficult jobs.

These girls sort ore in a copper mine in 1865. They are all in their early teens. By the time they are thirty years old, they will probably look as if they are fifty. Hard physical labor shortened lives and deformed the bodies of the young.

This young girl has come from Ireland to work as a "domestic" or maid for a well-to-do family. Some of these young people were treated as slaves. They worked night and day for next to nothing.

The early schools

In the early days children had no time to go to school. They had to help their parents on the farm. As a community grew more settled, people worked together to build a one-room school. Children of all ages were taught in one room by one teacher. The children learned the basics of reading, writing, and arithmetic.

Before the schoolhouse was built, children were taught to read at home. Mother takes time out of her busy day to read with Polly.

There was usually an educated woman in the community who took young children in to teach them to read. This kind of school was called a "dame school." Dame schools were replaced by one-room schools.

Some parents had to send their children to another town if they wanted them to have an education. These boys are boarding with a minister, who teaches them some basic subjects.

The opening of the village school was a happy event for these children. The whole community lent a hand to built its first school. Notice the tree stumps on the left. The wood in the schoolhouse came from the trees that were cut down on this land.

Even diseases such as the mumps can be fatal if they are treated in the wrong way.

This child is in a hospital with diphtheria. She has a very high temperature and is too weak even to look at her books. A kind nurse reads her a story.

Death – a part of settler life

Many children died before they were five years old. They died from illnesses which would be easily cured today. In the early days, it was often not the disease but the remedy which killed the patients. For example, when a baby was teething, the parents put leeches behind the baby's ears. Sometimes the gums were cut open to allow the new teeth to come through. Children died from whooping cough, measles, diphtheria, polio, scarlet fever, and rickets. One of the biggest problems was that people in those days did not know about good nutrition. They did not know what a big part fresh air, exercise, and cleanliness played in staying healthy. In the early days it was believed that bathing took away the natural oils which protected the body. Many infections were a result of not being clean.

The settlers had to face the possibility that their children might die. There were no cures for many diseases. Accepting death was made easier because of a strong belief that children would go to heaven. The story on the next page shows how a brother and sister coped with the death of their young sister.

Elisabeth is crippled from polio. There were no vaccinations against polio in those days. It was not unusual to find several crippled children in a community.

The three wishes

One winter evening three children sat around the fire. They were tired with play. It was too early to light candles. They had brought their chairs quite near the fire. They sat looking into the bright flames that danced up and down amongst the coals. Outside the window the rain was beating and the wind was howling. It was very pleasant to sit cosily by the fire while the weather was so rough outdoors.

The youngest, who was quite a tiny girl, looked up and said, "Why don't we talk?" "What shall we talk about?" the second child said, "Shall we make up stories, or play at being grown-up?" "I wish I was as big as papa," said the eldest. "Let us all wish!" cried the youngest little girl. "Oh! Do let us all wish!"

What do I want the most?

And so it was settled that they should think for five minutes by the mantel clock. Then they should say what they wished for most in the world. They all began to think very hard about what they would like best. A great many things they wished for came into their heads, and were pushed out again by other things that they seemed to wish more. The youngest thought of the beautiful doll, with blue eyes and long curly hair, that was under the glass case in the toy shop. At first, she wished for the doll. But before the five minutes were up she remembered her favorite story of "Puss-in-boots," and wished she had a cat in boots who was as clever as the one in the storybook. She remembered just in time that Mamma had said it wasn't a true story, and that there were no real cats like that. She was glad she had not told the others of her wish, because Tom would have laughed.

Then the five minutes came to an end, and little Nellie was not ready to say what she wished for. It turned out that the other two were not a bit more ready than she was, so they agreed to take ten minutes more. They all began to think harder than ever. Little Nellie found it quite difficult. She would have liked to be one of the princesses in the fairy tales, but there was just the same fault with that as with Puss-in-boots, so she had to give it up. At last, all in a minute, something came into her head. She remembered how Mamma had kissed her last night, just before she went to sleep, and had said, "God bless my Nellie, and make her good and happy!"

Nellie makes her choice

"I'll wish what Mamma wishes," thought Nellie. "That's sure to be right, and that means so much. Perhaps if I wish that, I might get the doll, or even Puss-in-boots. But no, that's not likely. But if I'm good, Mamma won't scold anymore." With a sigh of relief the little golden head sank against the back of the chair and Nellie waited patiently till the ten minutes had ended. At last the time was up, and Tom said, "Are you ready?"

The other two children said "Yes," and listened eagerly for Tom to tell them what he wished. "I should like to go away over the sea to foreign countries, where there are lions and bears. I should like to be a great man and fight battles and win them, and have people shout when they saw me come home."

And then the second child told her wish. "I should like to write a book, one that everybody should read, and to get a great deal of money - enough to build a hospital."

Then Nellie said, "I should like to be good and happy." The three children sat around the fire talking over their three wishes. In the meantime, something happened. Although none of them had known it, or even thought of it, each child's guardian angel had been near. As soon as the children had finished telling about their wishes, the angels spread out their great white wings and flew straight through the sky toward the most distant star. They flew up and up, until they reached heaven. They waited until they were given permission to speak, and then they told the Great Father the wishes of the children. And the Great Father told the angels to do what the children had asked. The angels flew down and down through the dark night, each with a message to fulfill.

"And then into the room came a child with golden hair."

44

Fifty years later...

Fifty years passed away. Once again the rain beat against the window and the wind howled amongst the trees. Inside the large house the firelight danced and flickered on the walls and furniture, bright with gold and rich silks. On one side of the hearth sat a tall man with white hair and a long white beard. He was reading a book. He looked very tired and ill. Beside him sat a lady, with a grave and quiet face. She sat looking into the fire, with her white hands clasped together on her lap. And then into the room came a child - a child with golden hair. She took a place between them. But they did not see her. They did not know she was so near to them, but they were thinking of her. The gentleman looked up at the picture of her over the mantelpiece - a picture of the very child who stood close by him. "Do you remember our wishes?" he said.

"Yes, I remember," the lady answered. And, just for a minute, the grand, bright room faded away, and they saw instead three children sitting around a fire. Then the lady spoke again. "You have had your wish. You have been across the sea to wild countries, and hunted lions and bears, and fought battles and won them. Today, when you came home, the streets were full of people, who shouted as you came. Has it made you happy?"

Have our wishes made us happy?

The gentleman shook his head sadly. He thought of two graves out in the distant country. His wife and child lay sleeping there, while he was alone. Besides, although he did not think of it, there was another reason he was miserable. All the time that he had been growing great and rich he had let his heart grow hard, proud, and cold. And so, though he had his wish, he felt he had nothing at all.

The lady spoke again. "I have had my wish. I wrote a book, and everybody read it, and money came - enough to build a hospital. Many sick people have blessed me for giving them health and strength once more." Then the gentleman

asked, "Are you happy?" She bowed her head as she answered, "I am content. My life has been very quiet, and sometimes very sad. I am growing old now, and till today when you came home, I have lived here always alone."

Nellie's heavenly choice

Then the gentleman pointed to the picture (though the child was standing close beside his knee he did not see her). "And what of her?" he said, "She wished to be good and happy." The lady looked up and smiled. "Surely she had her wish fifty years ago, when God took her away to be one of the angels that always stays by Him in heaven." "We did not think so then," said the gentleman, "Have you changed your mind?"

"We did not think she had her wish then," answered the lady. "We found her sleeping in her crib, with a smile on her face as if the angels had called her. But we never thought how happy she was, or that God would keep her always good. We only wanted to have Nellie back with us on earth. Would she have always been good and happy had she stayed with us on earth? Have we been so? Our wishes bound us to earth, but hers led her straight to heaven. She will be waiting for us there, and even now I know we have a child in heaven who loves us."

Still good and happy

While she spoke the figure of the golden-haired child grew brighter and clearer. The glistening white robe shone like the stars. And then the child glided across to the lady and kissed her forehead. The lady felt a little breath of wind touch her. Just then she thought of little Nellie, who still loved her in heaven. Then the child went to the old gentleman and put her hand softly on his heart. He did not know it, but as her hand touched him, all the proud, bad things that had gathered into his heart in those fifty years dropped away from him one by one. He grew humble and loving once more. Two tears rolled down his cheeks as he murmured gently, "Thank God that we have a child in heaven who loves us."

The minister's daughter showed William and Lucy the book which could tell their fortunes.

Living and learning from the Bible

Every settler home had a Bible. People read it every day. Children learned to recite verses from it. In fact, children had their very first reading lessons from the Bible. The settlers, both young and old, tried to live according to the Scriptures. People judged parents by the way their children behaved. Parents felt that as soon as a baby was born, the first lesson he or she had to learn was obedience. Values learned from the Bible, such as humility, industry, charity, courage, and honesty, were drilled into children in different ways. Every story a child read was loaded with morals and lessons. The settlers felt that children should read only to learn how to be "good." Reading for enjoyment was not permitted by many parents.

The story below appeared in a nineteenth-century children's magazine. It was written to show children that the Bible was a truly magic book.

The fortune-telling book

"I wish I had a fortune book," said one of three children who were walking down to the river for a swim. "I want to know what my luck is to be. I've tried to buy one, but there's none for sale."
"I have one," said the minister's daughter.
"Got one!" cried William eagerly. "Why did you not tell us about it before? Where is it?"
"Down at the church," answered the minister's daughter.
"And it does tell what's coming to pass, does it?" asked the third child, Lucy.
"Yes, it does."
"But how do you know?" asked Lucy. "You have not lived long enough to know if it has told your fortune right."
"Why, you see it is a very old book," said the minister's daughter. "My grandfather had it, and it told his fortune. Now my father has it, and it tells his."
"It beats all," cried William. "What a prize! Why don't you go around telling fortunes? You would make lots of money."
"I am afraid nobody would believe me," said the minister's daughter humbly.
"Well, show it to us," said the other two children.
"Come down to the church tonight, then," she said.

"Sell it to me," cried William.
"I cannot part with ours," answered the minister's daughter, "but you can get one where mine came from."
"I will have one! But we will come and try our luck with yours."
"Agreed," said the two girls.

A surprise ending

The minister's daughter invited the two children in and asked them to be seated. She drew a little table out and placed a lamp on it. Then she went to the back part of the church and, opening a little trunk (for, as you may well think, such a book was kept very carefully), took it out, and laid it on the table.

"There," she said, in a very serious tone. "There is my fortune-telling book. What it says is *sure*." The two friends eagerly gazed on the table and the book.

"The *Bible*!" they exclaimed, at once shrinking back. "Yes," said the minister's daughter, "that is my father's Bible. It says there are but two ways for me and you to try our chances in this world. One is called the "broad way," and the other the "straight and narrow way.""

Such a fortune-telling book the children were not thinking of. But it is the only kind that does not deceive us.

Melinda finds the words of the Bible a bit difficult to understand. However, she and Shep do not give up.

"Proper" pastimes

Settler parents felt that children should not engage in activities which interfered with their chores or made them physically or mentally tired. There were few "acceptable" pastimes. Parents felt gardening was a good way for children to spend their leisure time. It taught them to rise early, to share through making gifts of fruits and flowers, and to be orderly with weeding the garden.

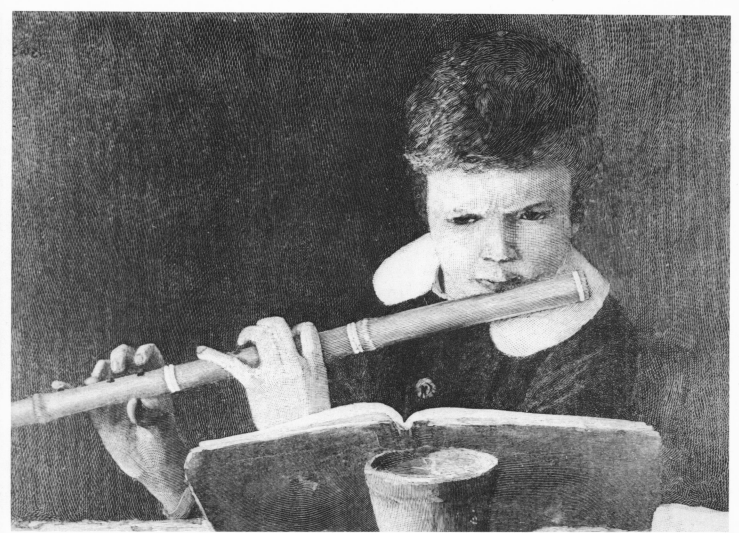

It was believed that children should learn to sing and to play at least one musical instrument. Lionel is not convinced that it is such a good idea.

Many people believed that playing cards was not a good activity for children. People felt it led to gambling. However, playing "with" cards was acceptable.

According to parents, the best activities for children were walking, riding, visiting, and reading. Parents thought that non-fiction books were more suitable for children to read because they would learn something during their spare time.

Almost all settler children had a pet of some sort. These children find this bear cub adorable. However, their parents are frightened to death. If Mamma Bear should happen to come around, these two little ones would be in a lot of trouble! Bears do not like anyone or anything to go near their cubs.

The birth of any new animal was an exciting event. These children are now the proud owners of three new puppies. These lovable puppies are wonderful to play with.

Playful pets

Children did not have much time to play once they were old enough to work. However, even the children who lived on farms found many happy ways to spend the little free time they were given. There were many animals on the farm. Each child had at least one or two pets with which he or she could share many happy moments.

Katherine loves to feed the birds every day. These little sparrows have become Katherine's friends.

Bunnies were a favorite pet then, as they are now. And five bunnies are definitely better than one.

Simple toys provided many pleasures

The early settlers did not have fancy toys to play with. Their parents and grandparents made the children's toys by hand. Grandma and Grandpa, above, want to surprise their grandchildren with a doll and a miniature farmhouse. Grandfather is whittling something right now. What do you think it might be?

These children are lucky to own a "Noah's Ark." Their grandfather carved the ark and the animals from wood. A Noah's Ark was the only toy children were allowed to play with on Sundays, because the story of Noah was a Bible story.

Children loved to play outdoors with a simple hoop and stick. Grandfather, who is the village cooper, is making a hoop for his grandchildren. Hoop races were exciting because the hoops were sure to take the wrong direction or fall flat on the grass.

children found boards and pieces of string exciting playthings. The boys have made a see-saw from a plank of wood and a stone. The girls are playing "cat's cradle" with a piece of string.

Simple toys, such as a piece of rope, allowed children to use their imaginations. The girls are reciting a skipping rhyme the girl in front skips to the beat.

"I'd rather have a real horse to ride, but I can have almost as much fun pretending." Settler children could make their own adventures with almost any object that was available.

Settler children enjoyed the outdoors in both winter and summer. In winter, they could sled, toboggan, snowshoe, and skate. These boys are going to play hockey. The two team captains are finding out who will choose a team member first.

The wonders of winter

The settler children loved the outdoors. They spent as much time outside as they could, both in winter and summer. Some of their favorite winter activities were sledding, tobogganing, snowshoeing, skating, sliding, snowballing, and going for rides in the family sleigh or cutter.

Maurice is proud of the wooden sled his father made. He is going to join his friends at the big hill for a day of fun in the snow.

Snowshoeing was a new sport for the settlers, but it became popular very quickly. Adrianne is ready for a long trek through the woods.

Playing at the old swimming hole was a great way to spend a lazy summer afternoon. Notice the bathing suits the girls are wearing.

The joys of summer

With his fishing rod and tackle
Slung aslant across his arm,
Phil went gaily to the river,
Down beyond the red-roofed farm.
Flung himself down beside a willow;
Breezes kissed his curly head,
While the dancing river murmured
          As it sped.

Children enjoyed simply being outside. These boys and girls are swinging on the gate. They exchange stories, sing songs, and pretend to be in faraway places.

Parlor fun and games

Settlers young and old, rich and poor, all loved *parlor games*. These games were called "parlor games" because they were usually played with guests. And guests were always entertained in the best room in the house - the parlor. Charades, "Blindman's Buff," and "Pin the Tail on the Donkey" are just a few of the games we still play today. Below are some of the older games that are not quite as well-known. Try playing them with your friends.

Twirling the plate

The players sit or stand around a table covered with a cloth. One of them takes up a wooden or metal plate, which sits on its edge. The player gives it a spin. As this is done, the player names one of the other players, who must catch the plate before it falls on the table, or else pay a penalty. The player called on sets the plate spinning in turn, calling upon some other player to stop it, and so on.

Cupid's coming

A letter must be taken, and the ending "ing." Say, for instance, the letter P is chosen. The first player says to the second, "Cupid's coming." "How is he coming?" says the second. "Playing," answers the first. The second then says to the third, "Cupid's coming." "How?" "Prancing." And so the question and reply go round, through all the words beginning with P and ending with "ing" - piping, pulling, pining, preaching. Those who cannot answer the question on the spur of the moment pay a penalty.

French blindman's buff

In French blindman's buff, the hands of the "blind" player are tied behind his or her back and the eyes are left uncovered. The player must therefore back onto the players in order to catch them, which increases the difficulties.

Blindman's wand

Here the blindfolded player has a stick. One end is grasped by the other players in turn. The "blind" player puts three questions to the other players. The aim is to recognize by the voice who it is that replies. The players, therefore, disguise their voices as much as possible. Sometimes, instead of merely asking the

Edith is waiting for her guests to arrive. She has planned an exciting day of parlor games for them. Join in on the fun!

Blindman's buff was a favorite parlor game. The child who was blindfolded was turned around several times. She then had to walk around, reaching out with her hands, until she caught someone.

After the "blind" player caught one of the other players, he had to identify that player by touch only. Andrew feels Birdie's face and hair and tries to guess who she is.

questions, the blind player instructs the holder of the wand to imitate some animal - a rooster or a donkey, for example.

Deer stalking

This is a game in which only two players take part, but it is exciting to watch. Both the "deer" and the "stalker" are blindfolded. They are then placed at opposite ends of a large table, and at a given moment begin to move around it. The stalker's business is, of course, to catch the deer, and the deer's to avoid it; but neither must run out into the room. Absolute silence should be kept both by the audience and players, and if slippers can be worn by both the deer and the stalker, so much the better.

Shadow games were both fun and a challenge. One had to place both hands in a certain way in order to make shadows of animals or things. Arnold has made a wolf with his fingers.

Children also played board games with their friends.

Imagination is one of the greatest gifts we have. Today we sometimes do not use it as much as we could because we have television, video games, and toys which do not require us to use our imaginations. In the days of the settlers, using imagination was often the only way children could have fun. The children, above, have opened a lemonade stand. They eagerly serve their first two customers.

Using their imaginations

A favorite game for settler children was "role playing." Children pretended to be mothers, fathers, blacksmiths, or storekeepers. They played at being people in the community. The children in this old picture are apothecaries, doctors, and patients. A game such as this could last for hours.

One of the best-loved ways to spend spare time was to give and accept challenges. One had to use one's imagination to come up with the challenge shown in this picture! The young man was the winner of the chair contest. No one could beat his spread!

Children pretended to be people from other times and places. Molly tries on grandmother's old hat and dress.

These children are rocking their sister on a chair. They are pretending that the chair is a see-saw.

Attitudes toward children changed in the late nineteenth century. Parents realized the need for children to play instead of work all the time. There was also more time for children to play. Much of the country was settled. Parents began to enjoy and even pamper their children. Many new toys were made in factories and could be bought in stores. Children owned huge doll houses, such as the one shown above. The doll houses were furnished one room at a time, piece by piece. The curtains were made by the children. Doll houses provided hours of imaginative play.

Time to play

Rocking horses were made of wood. They were very large compared to the ones children have today. The horse's tail was made of real horsehair.

Instead of cornhusk dolls, little girls began to play with fancy dolls made of porcelain and cloth. Toy doll carriages were made to look exactly like real ones.

Fancy dolls, doll carriages, train sets, and pieces of doll's furniture gave children many opportunities for play. Rosie prefers to read a new book. Even books were now more colorful and exciting.

These children can't wait to have a look inside the new kaleidoscope their father bought them. However, Father is so fascinated by the toy that he does not look ready to give it up.

The picture above was drawn from an 1890 photograph. By this time parents had a much different way of looking at their children. Parents doted on them and did not force them to grow up too quickly. These new parents are proud of their baby. They want to give him a happy childhood and a chance to be independent.

Change for children

The old ideas about how to be a good parent changed. The parents of the early nineteenth century could not wait to make children into adults. In the late nineteenth century, children were encouraged to enjoy their youth.

NEW RULES FOR PARENTS

1. Encourage your children to do well. Show them you are pleased when they do well.
2. Combine firmness with gentleness. Let your children understand that you mean exactly what you say.
3. Seldom threaten. Always be careful to keep your word.
4. Never punish your children when you are very angry. Be calm.
5. Never use violent or terrifying punishments.
6. Teach your children not to waste anything, to be clean and tidy, to sit quietly at meals, and to take care of and mend their clothes.
7. Above all, let parents be themselves what they would wish their children to be.

Glossary

almshouse *a place where poor people lived*

apothecary *a person who prepares and sells medicine; a druggist*

apprentice *a person who learns a trade or skill by working for a craftsperson*

baptism *a religious ceremony during which a person is sprinkled with water or dipped in water to show that the person's sins are washed away*

canvas *a heavy cloth*

christening *a religious ceremony during which a child is baptized and given a name*

community *a group of people living in the same area, sharing resources, public buildings, roads, and interests*

cooper *a person who makes wooden tubs and barrels*

cutter *a small sleigh usually pulled by one horse*

diphtheria *a disease which causes a fever, weakness, and difficulty in breathing*

domestic *a household servant, a maid; having to do with a house or household*

extended family *a family that includes parents, children, and other close relatives, such as grandparents, aunts and uncles*

fiction *written works, such as stories, that tell about characters and events which are not real*

flannel *a soft cloth made of wool or cotton*

flatiron *an iron heated by external heat, such as a fire, instead of from inside the iron*

godparent *a person who acts as a witness at a child's baptism and who promises to watch over the child's religious training*

gristmill *a mill that grinds up grain which farmers have grown*

herb *a plant or part of a plant used as medicine or to give flavor to food*

indenture *an agreement between people which requires one party to work for the other*

kaleidoscope *a moveable tube containing pieces of colored glass which form patterns at one end, and a hole at the other end to see the patterns through*

kindling *small pieces of wood used to start a fire*

leech *a worm which lives in water and sucks blood from other animals*

miller *a person who owns a mill, such as a gristmill*

moral *a lesson or message in a story which teaches good or right behavior*

muff *a tube of fur used to keep a person's hands warm*

mumps *a disease which causes the glands around the jaw to swell*

non-fiction *written works about real people and events*

ore *a mineral or rock containing a valuable substance, such as copper*

petticoat *an inner skirt or slip worn under an outer skirt*

pinafore *a garment without sleeves which looks like an apron*

polio *a disease which can cause paralysis, and sometimes death*

porcelain *a hard, white china made by baking clay at a high temperature*

reformatory *a place that is both a prison and a school for children who have broken the law*

rickets *a disease which deforms bones and is caused by a lack of Vitamin D*

sawmill *a factory where logs are cut into planks*

schooner *a sailing ship with two or more masts*

scriptures *religious writings in a holy book such as the Bible*

scythe *a tool with a long, curved blade and a long handle, used for cutting crops*

soup kitchen *a place where meals are offered free or for very little money*

steer *a young male cow raised for beef*

stowaway *a person who hides on a ship to get a free ride*

suspenders *a pair of straps worn around the shoulders to hold up a person's pants*

tonic *a medicine or liquid which refreshes or strengthens a person*

whooping cough *a disease which causes coughing and a blockage of the breathing passages in the body*

yoke *a bar with two U-shaped pieces put around the necks of oxen or other animals so that they pull or work together*

Index

Acknowledgements

Library of Congress, Dover Archives, Colonial Williamsburg, Century Village, Lang, Upper Canada Village, Black Creek Pioneer Village, Metropolitan Toronto Library, Colborne Lodge, Toronto Historical Board, Gibson House, City of North York, Harper's Weekly, Notman Photographic Archives, McCord Museum, City of Toronto Archives, Public Archives of Canada, Frank Leslie's Illustrated Magazine, Canadian Illustrated News, the Osborne Collection of Early Children's Books, Toronto Public Library, the Buffalo and Erie County Public Library Rare Book Department, Jamestown, Chatterbox, Little Wide Awake, Harper's Round Table Magazine, John P. Robarts Library, William Blackwood and Sons.

12131415 LB Printed in the U.S.A. 987654